Printed in the United States of America

First Printing, 2020

ISBN 978-0-578-84467-1

New York, NY

Dedication

For Eleanor and my beloved children

Go!

Go car.

Go truck.

Go bus.

Go taxi.

Go bike.

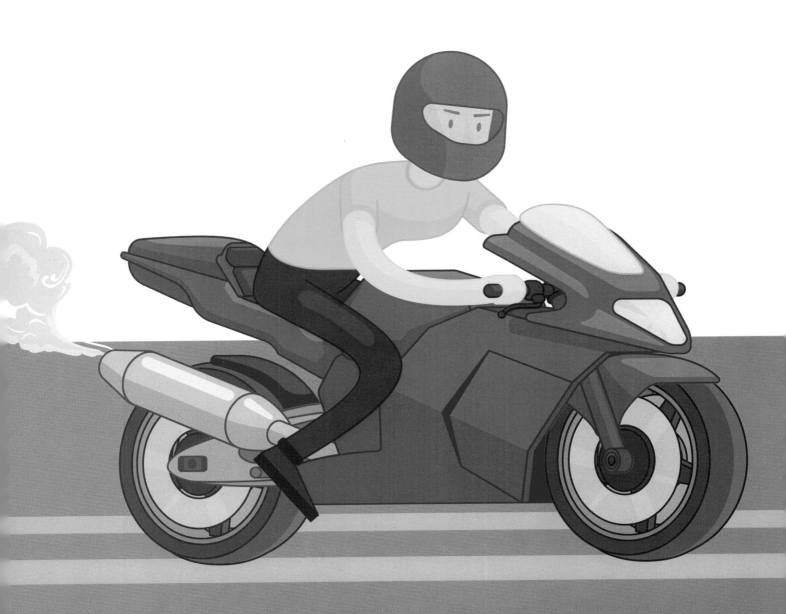

Go choo choo.

Go kitty.

Go doggy.

Go horsey.

Go piggy.

Go bunny.

Go ducky.

Go froggy.

Go Mommy.

Go Daddy.

Go baby.

You go.

I go.

Let's go

Go outside.

Biography for Baby Books

C. C. Franklin, a graduate of the University of Texas, is a speech-language pathologist, mom, and teacher specializing in early language development for children ages eighteen months to three years. She holds a Master of Arts in communication disorders and a Master of Fine Arts in creative writing and is a member of the American Speech and Hearing Association. She works with toddlers to expand receptive and expressive language skills and promote cognitive growth. Her interests include childhood literacy, health, and happiness.

The End